Copyright © 2013 by Todd Mikkelsen. All Rights Reserved.

No part of this document may be reproduced or transmitted in any form or by any means, electronic, mechanical, photocopying, recording, or otherwise, without prior written permission of Todd Mikkelsen, except by a reviewer, who may quote short passages in a review where suitable.

Preface

I was personally contacted by several fans, via e-mail, encouraging me to write a proper quick , fast, rapid, etc. deploy bracelet book. The things requested... make sure the bracelets can truly deploy quickly, have simple stopper knots, don't singe the ends for access to the core strands, and get more paracord into the bracelet than the average design.

Below are links to my blog and YouTube Channel:

> http://paracord101.blogspot.com/

> http://tiny.cc/auxdtw

What do you need to make the bracelets in this book? A ruler, scissors, paracord, patience, and learn from mistakes that are made.

Some of the bracelets in this book are inspired by things I am personally interested in: Sasquatch, Noodling, Prepper, Bug Out Bags, etc.

Why Sasquatch? In late November of 2003 at roughly 10:30 PM with subzero temperatures in Austin, MN I was reading in bed. My bedroom was on the north side of the house. Suddenly, the entire house shook as if it were an earthquake. I feared for my families safety. The scientist in me needed to investigate what had just happened. I grabbed a high beam flashlight and headed outside with an unzipped winter jacket, t-shirt, jeans, and untied snow boots. The wind was calm and I could hear cars driving in the distance. There was roughly 8 inches of snow on the ground. At the time, I had no landscaping in my yard and no other houses were around mine in the housing development. This created a wind tunnel effect for drifting. Also, the south lot next to mine had a 8 feet all culvert that was removed the summer of 2003. Could it have been a resting spot for a Bigfoot? For a brief time, it was like living in the country... isolated and desolate. I walked around the perimeter of my house. I discovered giant tracks leading up to the master bedroom window on the north side of the house. There was a fresh dent in the vinyl siding. Here was the epicenter. The tracks back tracked toward a snow drift, produced by the recent snowstorm, in my back yard. The drift was up to my waist. I am 6 feet, 2 inches tall. I clearly saw a bipedal set of tracks through the drift. The snow was not plowed through. I could see that the animal's long legs had gone in and back out of the holes. I followed the tracks for another one hundred feet to the street. I stood there pointing the flashlight randomly at the row of pine trees that lined the street. I paused knowing that something larger than myself was outside with me. Then... I heard it. Rumph! Rumph! Rumph! Whatever was making that noise sounded like a primate, sounded like it was cold, and was getting closer. I could also see the pine trees move as if a large animal was walking slowly toward me. I pivoted around and ran as quickly as I could back to my house. That night I became a believer in Sasquatch, a.k.a. Bigfoot. In late March of 2004, a similar earth shaking thud shook my house a second time. I again went outside with the same high beam flashlight and found a new dent on the south side of my vinyl siding. Do Bigfeet migrate with the changing weather? The dents on my siding may be a clue to if they do or not.

Table of Contents

Knife Lanyard Knot — 1

Double Oysterman's Stopper Knot — 2

Zipper Sinnet — 3

Thick Zipper Sinnet — 5

Ripcord Sinnet — 6

Hitched Ripcord Sinnet — 9

Chimera Sinnet — 12

Squatch Sinnet — 15

Exploding Brainworm Sinnet — 18

Noodlin Sinnet — 22

Bug Out Sinnet — 26

Paisley Sinnet — 30

Divine Ridgeback Sinnet — 35

Chained Zipper Sinnet — 38

Gator Tail Sinnet — 42

Gatorback Sinnet — 45

S.H.T.F. Sinnet — 49

STOPPER KNOTS

KNIFE LANYARD KNOT

The knife lanyard knot (a.k.a. diamond knot) makes a good decorative stopper knot. It is made with a Carrick Bend and a series of bends that go through the center of the knot.

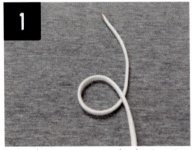
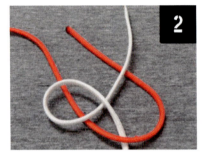
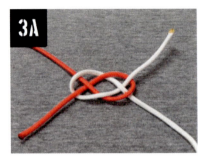

1. Make a counter-clockwise **9**.
2. Place the left cord under the **9**, over the long end, and tuck under the short end of the **9**.
3A. Tuck the ends under the long ends of the opposing cords to create a Carrick Bend.

3B. Close up of the Carrick Bend.
4. The right cord is pulled for more slack.
5. Pull the short end of the right cord to reduce slack.

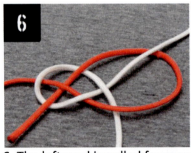

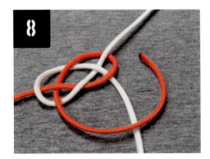

6. The left cord is pulled for more slack.
7. Pull the short end of the left cord to reduce slack.
8. Make a bend with the left cord over the long end of the right cord.

9. Pull the end of the left cord through the center.
10. Make a bend with the right cord over the long end of the left cord.
11. Pull the end of the right cord through the center and tighten the knot.

«««««««««««««««««««««««««««««««««««»»»»»»»»»»»»»»»»»»»»»»»»»»»»»»»»»»»»»»»

DOUBLE OYSTERMAN'S STOPPER KNOT

The Oysterman's Stopper Knot is a simple stopper knot that is easy to untie for most quick deploy sinnets.

 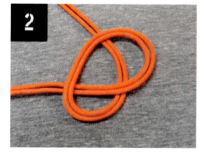 

1. Make a counter-clockwise bend.
2. Pull the short end under the bend.
3. Thread the short end through the bottom loop.

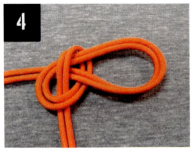  

4. Slightly tighten the knot.
5. Pull the working end of the cords through the loop on the right and tighten.

««««««««««««««««««««««««««««««««««««»»

QUICK DEPLOY SINNETS

ZIPPER SINNET

The Zipper Sinnet is a historical tie that can be easily and quickly deployed in a matter of seconds.

Sinnet Material Equation: 7 feet cord = 7.25 inch bracelet

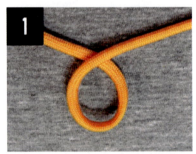  

1. Make a loop, clockwise *O* from left to right, in the middle of the cord.
2. Bend and pull the left cord through the loop.
3. Tighten the knot and adjust the cord to make a 0.5 inch loop. The loop should be slightly larger than the stopper knot of your choice.

4. Make a loop with the right cord.
5. Bend and pull the left cord through the loop on the right.
6. Tighten the knot and adjust the cord to make a small loop.

7. Bend and pull the right cord through the loop on the left.
8. Tighten the knot and adjust the cord to make a small loop.
9. Bend and pull the left cord through the loop on the right.

10. Tighten the knot and adjust the cord to make a small loop.
11. Bend and pull the right cord through the loop on the left.
12. Tighten the knot and adjust the cord to make a small loop.

13. Continue the pattern to the desired length.
14. Insert both cord ends through the loop.
15. Tighten the last loop to secure the cord ends.

16. Make a Stopper Knot (refer to pages 1 through 3) for rapid deployment, cut the ends and do NOT singe. Leave ends open for quick access to the core strands.

THICK ZIPPER SINNET

The Thick Zipper Sinnet doubles the historical Zipper Sinnet allowing the wearer to have twice as much cord as the original.

Sinnet Material Equation: Two 7 feet cords = 7.25 inch bracelet

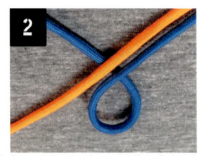

1. Make a loop, clockwise **O** from left to right, in the middle of the dark cord.
2. Lay the middle of the second light cord next to the loop.
3. Bend and pull the left dark cord over the second light cord and through the loop.

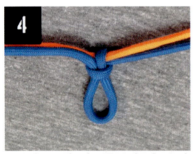

4. Tighten the knot and adjust the cord to make a 0.5 inch loop.
5. Make a counter-clockwise loop with the right cords.
6. Bend and pull the left cords through the loops on the right.

7. Tighten the knot and adjust the cords to make a small loop. Fine-tune the cords as needed.
8. Bend and pull the right cords through the loops on the left.
9. Tighten the knot and adjust the cords to make a small loop.

10. Bend and pull the left cords through the loops on the right.
11. Tighten the knot and adjust the cords to make a small loop.
12. Continue the pattern to the desired length.

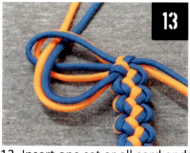  

13. Insert one set or all cord ends through the loop.
14. Tighten the last loop to secure the cord ends.
15. Make a Stopper Knot (refer to pages 1 through 3), cut the ends and do NOT singe. Leave ends open for quick access to the core strands.

«««««««««««««««««««««««««««««««««««««»»»»»»»»»»»»»»»»»»»»»»»»»»»»»»»»»»»»

RIPCORD SINNET

The Ripcord Sinnet is THE pioneering and modern quick deploy sinnet created by JD Lenzen. Its structure allows for a respectable amount of cord to be stored in a small space. This sinnet uses a series of slip knots synched together.

Sinnet Material Equation: 12 feet cord = 7.25 inch bracelet

1. Make a loop, clockwise *O* from left to right, in the middle of the cord.
2. Bend then pull the left cord through the loop.
3. Tighten the slip knot and adjust the cord to make a 0.5 inch loop.

4. Make a counter-clockwise loop with the right cord then bend and pull the left cord through the loop on the right.
5. Tighten the knot and make a small loop.
6. Make a counter-clockwise loop with the right cord then bend and pull the right cord over and through itself.

7. Tighten the slip knot and make a small loop.
8. Pull the right slip knot through the left loop.
9. Tighten the left cord.

10. Make a clockwise loop with the left cord then bend and pull the left cord over and through itself.
11. Tighten the slip knot and make a small loop.
12. Pull the left slip knot through the right loop.

13. Tighten the right cord.
14. Make a counter-clockwise loop with the right cord then bend and pull the right cord over and through itself.
15. Tighten the slip knot and make a small loop.

16. Pull the right slip knot through the left loop.
17. Tighten the left cord.
18. Make a clockwise loop with the left cord then bend and pull the left cord over and through itself.

19. Tighten the slip knot and make a small loop.
20. Pull the left slip knot through the right loop.
21. Tighten the right cord.

22. Continue the pattern to the desired length.
23. Insert both cord ends through the loop.
24. Tighten the last loop to secure the cord ends.

25. Make a Stopper Knot (refer to pages 1 through 3), cut the ends and do NOT singe. Leave ends open for quick access to the core strands.

«««»»

HITCHED RIPCORD SINNET

The Hitched Ripcord Sinnet is a variation of the Ripcord Sinnet. The design uses a half hitch prior to the slip knot.

Sinnet Material Equation: 11 feet cord = 7.25 inch bracelet

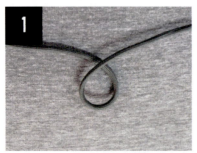 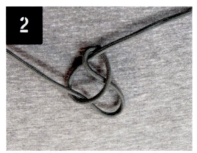 

1. Make a, clockwise *O* from left to right, loop in the middle of the cord.
2. Bend and pull the left cord through the loop.
3. Tighten the slip knot and adjust the cord to make a 0.5 inch loop.

4. Make a counter-clockwise loop with the right cord then bend and pull the left cord through the loop on the right. Tighten the knot and make a small loop.
5. Make a counter-clockwise loop with the right cord then bend and pull the right cord over and through itself.
6. Tighten the knot.

7. Pull the right slip knot through the left loop.
8. Tighten the left cord.
9. Wrap the left cord around the right loop and through itself to create a half-hitch.

  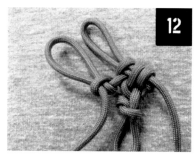

10. Tighten the half-hitch knot.
11. Make a clockwise loop with the left cord then bend and pull the left cord over and through itself.
12. Tighten the slip knot and make a small loop.

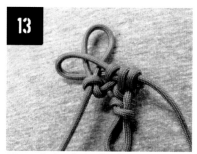 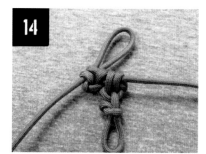 

13. Pull the left slip knot through the right loop.
14. Tighten the right cord.
15. Wrap the right cord around the left loop and through itself to create a half-hitch.

16. Tighten the half-hitch knot.
17. Make a counter-clockwise loop with the right cord then bend and pull the right cord over and through itself.
18. Tighten the slip knot and make a small loop.

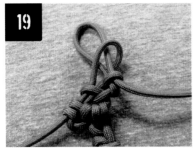  

19. Pull the right slip knot through the left loop.
20. Tighten the left cord.
21. Wrap the left cord around the right loop and through itself to create a half-hitch.

22. Tighten the half-hitch knot.
23. Make a clockwise loop with the left cord then bend and pull the left cord over and through itself.
24. Tighten the slip knot and make a small loop.

25. Pull the left slip knot through the right loop.
26. Tighten the right cord.
27. Continue the pattern to the desired length.

28. Insert both cord ends through the loop.
29. Tighten the last loop to secure the cord ends.
30. Make a Stopper Knot (refer to pages 1 through 3), cut the ends and do NOT singe. Leave ends open for quick access to the core strands.

««»»»

CHIMERA SINNET

The term CHIMERA in modern folklore is used to describe a fictional beast with parts taken from different animals or creatures. The CHIMERA SINNET uses parts of various sinnets, a series of half-hitches and zipper sinnets, to craft a unique texture.

Sinnet Material Equation: 11 feet cord = 7.25 inch bracelet

1. Make a loop, clockwise *O* from left to right, in the middle of the cord.
2. Bend and pull the left cord through the loop.
3. Tighten the slip knot and adjust the cord to make a 0.5 inch loop.

4. Make a loop with the right cord, bend and pull the left cord through the loop on the right.
5. Tighten the knot and make a small loop.
6. Coil the right cord in a counter-clockwise direction around the left loop to create a half hitch.

7. Tighten the knot.
8. Bend and pull the right cord through the loop on the left.
9. Tighten the knot, adjust the cord to make a small loop and reduce the slack from the new loop.

10. Coil the left cord in a clockwise direction around the right loop to create a half hitch.
11. Tighten the knot.
12. Coil the left cord in a clockwise direction around the right loop to create a half hitch.

13. Tighten the knot.
14. Bend and pull the left cord through the loop on the right.
15. Tighten the knot, adjust the cord to make a small loop and reduce the slack from the new loop.

16. Coil the right cord in a counter-clockwise direction around the left loop to create a half hitch.
17. Tighten the knot.
18. Coil the right cord in a counter-clockwise direction around the left loop to create a half hitch.

19. Tighten the knot.
20. Bend and pull the right cord through the loop on the left.
21. Tighten the knot, adjust the cord to make a small loop and reduce the slack from the new loop.

22. Coil the left cord in a clockwise direction around the right loop to create a half hitch.
23. Tighten the knot.
24. Coil the left cord in a clockwise direction around the right loop to create a half hitch.

25. Tighten the knot.
26. Bend and pull the left cord through the loop on the right.
27. Tighten the knot, adjust the cord to make a small loop and reduce the slack from the new loop.

28. Continue the pattern to the desired length.
29. Insert both cord ends through the loop.
30. Tighten the last loop to secure the cord ends.

31. Make a Stopper Knot (refer to pages 1 through 3), cut the ends and do NOT singe. Leave ends open for quick access to the core strands.

«««««««««««««««««««««««««««««««««»»»»»»»»»»»»»»»»»»»»»»»»»»»»»»»»»

'SQUATCH SINNET

Gone Squatchin'? When one goes Squatchin', or Sasquatch hunting, with a video camera and audio recorder, one must be prepared for all types of weather conditions and terrain. The 'Squatch Sinnet has a reasonable amount of paracord in a small space due to its construction.

Sinnet Material Equation: 12 feet cord = 7.25 inch bracelet

1. Make a loop, counter-clockwise **O** from right to left, in the middle of the cord.
2. Bend and pull the right cord through the loop.
3. Tighten the slip knot and adjust the cord to make a 0.5 inch loop.

4. Make a loop with the right cord, bend and pull the left cord through the loop on the right.
5. Tighten the knot and make a small loop.
6. Coil the right cord twice in a counter-clockwise direction.

7. Bend and pull the right cord over and through the two coils.
8. Tighten the knot.
9. Pull the left loop through the right loop.

10. Tighten the knot on the right.
11. Bend and pull the right cord through the loop on the left.
12. Tighten the left cord and reduce the slack from the new loop.

13. Coil the left cord twice in a clockwise direction.
14. Bend and pull the left cord over and through the two coils.
15. Tighten the knot.

16. Pull the right loop through the left loop.
17. Tighten the knot on the left.
18. Bend and pull the left cord through the loop on the right.

19. Tighten the right cord and reduce the slack from the new loop.
20. Coil the right cord twice in a counter-clockwise direction.
21. Bend and pull the right cord over and through the two coils.

22. Tighten the knot.
23. Pull the left loop through the right loop.
24. Tighten the knot on the right.

25. Bend and pull the right cord through the loop on the left.
26. Tighten the left cord and reduce the slack from the new loop.
27. Coil the left cord twice in a clockwise direction.

28. Bend and pull the left cord over and through the two coils.
29. Tighten the knot.
30. Pull the right loop through the left loop.

31. Tighten the knot on the right.
32. Bend and pull the left cord through the loop on the right.
33. Tighten the right cord and reduce the slack from the new loop.

34. Continue the pattern to the desired length.
35. Insert both cord ends through the loop.
36. Tighten the last loop to secure the cord ends.

37. Make a Stopper Knot (refer to pages 1 through 3), cut the ends and do NOT singe. Leave ends open for quick access to the core strands.

«««««««««««««««««««««««««««««««««««»»»»»»»»»»»»»»»»»»»»»»»»»»»»»»»»»»»»»»

EXPLODING BRAINWORM SINNET

The EXPLODING BRAINWORM SINNET adds a slip-knot to the paracord bracelet design BRAINWORM SINNET created by JD Lenzen. This sinnet is made with a series of slip knots, half-hitches, and zipper sinnets.

Sinnet Material Equation: 11 feet cord = 7.25 inch bracelet

1. Make a loop, clockwise *O* from left to right, in the middle of the cord.
2. Bend and pull the left cord through the loop.
3. Tighten the slip knot and adjust the cord to make a 0.5 inch loop.

4. Make a loop with the right cord, bend and pull the left cord through the loop on the right.
5. Tighten the knot and make a small loop.
6. Make a counter-clockwise loop with the right cord then bend and pull the right cord over and through itself.

7. Tighten the knot.
8. Pull the left slip knot through the right loop.
9. Tighten the knot on the right.

10. Coil the right cord in a counter-clockwise direction around the left loop to create a half hitch.
11. Tighten the knot.
12. Bend and pull the right cord through the loop on the left.

13. Tighten the cord on the left.
14. Make a clockwise loop with the left cord then bend and pull the left cord over and through itself.
15. Tighten the knot.

16. Pull the right slip knot through the left loop.
17. Tighten the cord on the left.
18. Coil the left cord in a clockwise direction around the right loop to create a half hitch.

19. Tighten the knot.
20. Bend and pull the left cord through the loop on the right.
21. Tighten the cord on the right.

22. Make a counter-clockwise loop with the right cord then bend and pull the right cord over and through itself.
23. Tighten the knot.
24. Pull the left slip knot through the right loop.

25. Tighten the knot on the right.
26. Coil the right cord in a counter-clockwise direction around the left loop to create a half hitch.
27. Tighten the knot.

28. Bend and pull the right cord through the loop on the left.
29. Tighten the cord on the left.
30. Make a clockwise loop with the left cord then bend and pull the left cord over and through itself.

31. Tighten the knot.
32. Pull the right slip knot through the left loop.
33. Tighten the knot on the left.

34. Coil the left cord in a clockwise direction around the right loop to create a half hitch.
35. Tighten the knot.
36. Bend and pull the left cord through the loop on the right.

37. Tighten the cord on the right.
38. Continue the pattern to the desired length.
39. Insert both cord ends through the loop.

40. Tighten the last loop to secure the cord ends.
41. Make a Stopper Knot (refer to pages 1 through 3), cut the ends and do NOT singe. Leave ends open for quick access to the core strands.

«««««««««««««««««««««««««««««««««»»»»»»»»»»»»»»»»»»»»»»»»»»»»»»»»»»»»»
NOODLIN' SINNET

Noodlin', or Noodling, is the practice of fishing for catfish using only bare hands or feet with socks. The noodler will place one's hand or socked foot inside as bait in a known catfish hole to catch a catfish. The NOODLIN' SINNET is a good length of cord that could be quickly deployed for stringing a catfish once it has been caught.

Sinnet Material Equation: 11 feet cord = 7.25 inch bracelet

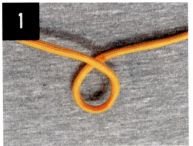  

1. Make a loop, clockwise **O** from right to left, in the middle of the cord.
2. Bend and pull the right cord through the loop.
3. Tighten the slip knot and adjust the cord to make a 0.5 inch loop.

4. Make a loop with the right cord, bend and pull the left cord through the loop on the right.
5. Tighten the knot and make a small loop.
6. Make a counter-clockwise loop with the right cord then bend and pull the right cord over and through itself.

7. Tighten the knot.
8. Pull the left slip knot through the right loop.
9. Tighten the slip knot on the right.

10. Bend and pull the right cord through the loop on the left.
11. Tighten the cord on the left and reduce the slack from the new loop.
12. Make a clockwise loop with the left cord then bend and pull the left cord over and through itself.

13. Tighten the knot.
14. Pull the right slip knot through the left loop.
15. Tighten the slip knot on the left.

16. Bend and pull the left cord through the loop on the right.
17. Tighten the right cord and reduce the slack from the new loop.
18. Make a counter-clockwise loop with the right cord then bend and pull the right cord over and through itself.

19. Tighten the knot.
20. Pull the left slip knot through the right loop.
21. Tighten the slip knot on the right.

22. Bend and pull the right cord through the loop on the left.
23. Tighten the cord on the right and reduce the slack from the new loop.
24. Make a clockwise loop with the left cord then bend and pull the left cord over and through itself.

25. Tighten the knot.
26. Pull the right slip knot through the left loop.
27. Tighten the slip knot on the left.

28. Bend and pull the left cord through the loop on the right.
29. Tighten the cord on the right and reduce the slack from the new loop.
30. Continue the pattern to the desired length.

31. Insert both cord ends through the loop.
32. Tighten the last loop to secure the cord ends.
33. Make a Stopper Knot (refer to pages 1 through 3), cut the ends and do NOT singe. Leave ends open for quick access to the core strands.

BUG OUT SINNET

A bug-out-bag is typically a back pack that contains items one would need to survive for three days when evacuating from a natural or man-made disaster. The BUG OUT SINNET provides enough paracord one would need in case an emergency arouse; tourniquet, sling for a broken arm, broken pack strap, etc.

Sinnet Material Equation: 14 feet cord = 7.25 inch bracelet

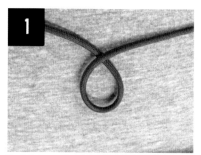
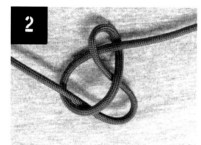
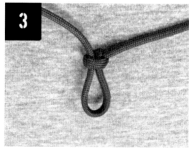

1. Make a loop, clockwise *O* from left to right, in the middle of the cord.
2. Bend and pull the left cord through the loop.
3. Tighten the slip knot and adjust the cord to make a 0.5 inch loop.

4. Make a loop with the right cord, bend and pull the left cord through the loop on the right.
5. Tighten the knot and make a small loop.
6. Make a counter-clockwise loop with the right cord then bend and pull the right cord over and through itself.

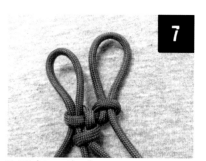

7. Tighten the knot.
8. Pull the left slip knot through the right loop.
9. Tighten the right slip knot.

10. Make a counter-clockwise loop with the right cord then bend and pull the right cord over and through itself.
11. Tighten the knot.
12. Bend and pull the right cord through the loop.

13. Tighten the cord by reducing the slack from the new loop.
14. Pull the right slip knot through the left loop.
15. Tighten the cord on the left.

16. Make a clockwise loop with the left cord then bend and pull the left cord over and through itself.
17. Tighten the knot.
18. Pull the right slip knot through the left loop.

19. Tighten the slip knot on the left.
20. Make a clockwise loop with the left cord then bend and pull the left cord over and through itself.
21. Tighten the knot.

22. Bend and pull the left cord through the loop.
23. Tighten the cord by reducing the slack from the new loop.
24. Pull the left slip knot through the right loop.

25. Tighten the cord on the right.
26. Make a counter-clockwise loop with the right cord then bend and pull the right cord over and through itself.
27. Tighten the knot.

28. Pull the left slip knot through the right loop.
29. Tighten the slip knot on the right.
30. Make a counter-clockwise loop with the right cord then bend and pull the right cord over and through itself.

31. Tighten the knot.
32. Bend and pull the right cord through the loop on the left.
33. Tighten the cord by reducing the slack from the new loop.

34. Pull the right slip knot through the left loop.
35. Tighten the cord on the left.
36. Make a clockwise loop with the left cord then bend and pull the left cord over and through itself.

37. Tighten the knot.
38. Pull the right slip knot through the left loop.
39. Tighten the slip knot on the left.

40. Make a clockwise loop with the left cord then bend and pull the left cord over and through itself.
41. Tighten the knot.
42. Bend and pull the left cord through the loop.

43. Tighten the cord by reducing the slack from the new loop.
44. Pull the left slip knot through the right loop.
45. Tighten the cord on the right.

46. Continue the pattern to the desired length.
47. Insert both cord ends through the loop.
48. Tighten the last loop to secure the cord ends.

49. Make a Stopper Knot (refer to pages 1 through 3), cut the ends and do NOT singe. Leave ends open for quick access to the core strands.

«««««««««««««««««««««««««««««««««««««»»»»»»»»»»»»»»»»»»»»»»»»»»»»»»»»»»»»»»

PAISLEY SINNET

The PAISLEY SINNET pattern creates a hole that resembles a paisley design. This sinnet surprisingly holds a good amount of paracord in its structure.

Sinnet Material Equation: 15 feet cord = 7.25 inch bracelet

1. Make a loop, clockwise **O** from right to left, in the middle of the cord.
2. Bend and pull the right cord through the loop.
3. Tighten the slip knot and adjust the cord to make a 0.5 inch loop.

4. Make a loop with the right cord, bend and pull the left cord through the loop on the right.
5. Tighten the knot and make a small loop.
6. Make a counter-clockwise loop with the right cord then bend and pull the right cord over and through itself.

7. Tighten the knot.
8. Pull the left loop through the right slip knot.
9. Tighten the right slip knot.

10. Make a counter-clockwise loop with the right cord then bend and pull the right cord over and through itself.
11. Tighten the knot.
12. Pull the left loop through the right slip knot.

13. Tighten the right slip knot.
14. Make a counter-clockwise loop with the right cord then bend and pull the right cord over and through itself.
15. Tighten the knot.

16. Pull the left loop through the right slip knot.
17. Tighten the right slip knot.
18. Make a counter-clockwise loop with the right cord then bend and pull the right cord over and through itself.

19. Tighten the knot.
20. Pull the left loop through the right slip knot.
21. Tighten the right slip knot.

22. Bend and pull the right cord through the loop on the left.
23. Tighten the cord on the left and reduce the slack from the new loop.
24. Make a clockwise loop with the left cord then bend and pull the left cord over and through itself.

25. Tighten the knot.
26. Pull the right loop through the left slip knot.
27. Tighten the slip knot on the left.

28. Make a clockwise loop with the left cord then bend and pull the left cord over and through itself.
29. Tighten the knot.
30. Pull the right loop through the left slip knot.

31. Tighten the left slip knot.
32. Make a clockwise loop with the left cord then bend and pull the left cord over and through itself.
33. Tighten the slip knot.

34. Pull the right loop through the left slip knot.
35. Tighten the left slip knot.
36. Make a clockwise loop with the left cord then bend and pull the left cord over and through itself.

37. Tighten the knot.
38. Pull the right loop through the left slip knot.
39. Tighten the left slip knot.

40. Bend and pull the left cord through the loop on the right.
41. Tighten the cord on the left and reduce the slack from the new loop.
42. Continue the pattern to the desired length.

43. Make a slip knot to even out the stress of the cord and keep the pattern. Make a clockwise loop with the left cord then bend and pull the left cord over and through itself.
44. Tighten the slip knot.
45. Pull the right loop through the left slip knot.

46. Tighten the left slip knot.
47. Insert both cord ends through the loop.
48. Tighten the last loop to secure the cord ends.

49. Make a Stopper Knot (refer to pages 1 through 3), cut the ends and do NOT singe. Leave ends open for quick access to the core strands.

DIVINE RIDGEBACK SINNET

The DIVINE RIDGEBACK SINNET is named after the Rhodesian Ridgeback dog bred in South Africa. The Rhodesian Ridgeback has a unique fur ridge on its back that runs in the opposite direction from the rest of its coat. This sinnet is made with an interlocking zipper sinnet with a series of slip knots. The zipper sinnet (shown here with the light cord) is key to quickly unraveling this sinnet.

Sinnet Material Equation: One 10 feet light cord + One 12 feet dark cord = 7.25 inch bracelet

  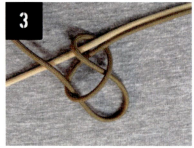

1. Make a loop, clockwise *O* from left to right, in the middle of the dark cord.
2. Lay the middle of the second light cord next to the loop.
3. Bend then pull the left dark cord over the second light cord and through the loop.

4. Tighten the knot and adjust the cord to make a 0.5 inch loop.
5. Make a counter-clockwise loop with the right light cord, bend and pull the left light cord through the loop on the right.
6. Tighten the knot and make a small loop.

7. Make a counter-clockwise loop with the right dark cord then bend and pull the right cord over and through itself.
8. Tighten the knot.
9. Pull the left light loop through the right dark loop.

10. Tighten the right dark slip knot.
11. Bend and pull the right light cord through the loop on the left.
12. Tighten the left light cord.

13. Make a clockwise loop with the left dark cord then bend and pull the right cord over and through itself.
14. Tighten the knot.
15. Pull the right light loop through the left dark loop.

16. Tighten the left dark slip knot.
17. Bend and pull the left lighter cord through the light loop on the right.
18. Tighten the light cord on the right.

19. Make a counter-clockwise loop with the right dark cord then bend and pull the right cord over and through itself.
20. Tighten the knot.
21. Pull the left light loop through the right dark loop.

  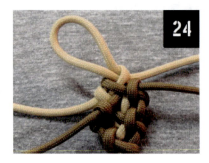

22. Tighten the right dark slip knot.
23. Bend and pull the right lighter cord through the light loop on the left.
24. Tighten the light cord on the left.

25. Turn the bracelet over to check the design...
26. With the working side...make a clockwise loop with the left dark cord then bend and pull the right cord over and through itself.
27. Tighten the knot.

28. Pull the right light loop through the left dark loop.
29. Tighten the left dark slip knot.
30. Continue the pattern to the desired length.

31. Insert the cord ends through the loop.
32. Tighten the last loop to secure the cord ends.
33. Make a Stopper Knot (refer to pages 1 through 3), cut the ends and do NOT singe. Leave ends open for quick access to the core strands.

«««««««««««««««««««««««««««««««««««««««»»

CHAINED ZIPPER SINNET

The CHAINED ZIPPER SINNET is a variation of the DIVINE RIDGEBACK SINNET. The zipper sinnet is made at a 90° angle, or pulled vertical, to the slip knot creating a chain-like appearance for the sinnet. The zipper sinnet is key to quickly unraveling this sinnet.

Sinnet Material Equation: One 10 feet light cord + One 12 feet dark cord = 7.25 inch bracelet

 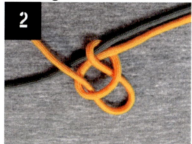 

1. Make a loop, clockwise **O** from left to right, in the middle of the light cord. Lay the middle of the second dark cord next to the loop.
2. Bend then pull the left light cord over the second dark cord and through the loop.
3. Tighten the knot and adjust the cord to make a 0.5 inch loop.

4. Make a loop with the right light cord, bend and pull the left light cord through the loop on the right.
5. Tighten the knot and make a small loop.
6. Make a clockwise loop with the left dark cord then bend and pull the right cord over and through itself.

7. Tighten the knot.
8. With the left dark cord, lasso the light cord loop.
9. Tighten the left dark slip knot. To create the chain pattern, pull the light cord vertically, a 90 degree angle to the sides, or toward yourself.

10. Make a counter-clockwise loop with the left dark cord then bend and pull the right cord over and through itself.
11. Tighten the knot.
12. With the right dark cord, lasso the light cord loop.

13. Tighten the right dark slip knot.
14. Bend and pull the bottom light cord through the light loop in the middle.
15. Tighten the top light cord and adjust the cord to vertical as needed.

16. Bend and pull the top light cord through the light loop in the middle.
17. Tighten the bottom light cord and adjust the cord to vertical as needed.
18. Make a clockwise loop with the left dark cord then bend and pull the right cord over and through itself.

19. Tighten the knot.
20. With the left dark cord, lasso the light cord loop.
21. Tighten the left slip knot.

22. Make a counter-clockwise loop with the right dark cord then bend and pull the right cord over and through itself.
23. Tighten the knot.
24. With the right dark cord, lasso the light cord loop.

25. Tighten the right dark slip knot.
26. Bend and pull the top light cord through the light loop in the middle.
27. Tighten the bottom light cord and adjust the cord to vertical as needed.

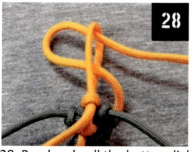  

28. Bend and pull the bottom light cord through the light loop in the middle.
29. Tighten the top light cord and adjust the cord to vertical as needed.
30. Make a clockwise loop with the left dark cord then bend and pull the right cord over and through itself.

31. Tighten the knot.
32. With the left dark cord, lasso the light cord loop.
33. Tighten the left slip knot.

34. Make a clockwise loop with the left dark cord then bend and pull the right cord over and through itself.
35. Tighten the knot.
36. With the right dark cord, lasso the light cord loop.

37. Bend and pull the top light cord through the light loop in the middle.
38. Tighten the bottom light cord and adjust the cord to vertical as needed.
39. Bend and pull the bottom light cord through the light loop in the middle.

40. Tighten the bottom light cord and adjust the cord to vertical as needed and continue the pattern to the desired length.
41. Insert the cord ends through the loop.
42. Tighten the last loop to secure the cord ends.

43. Make a Stopper Knot (refer to pages 1 through 3), cut the ends and do NOT singe. Leave ends open for quick access to the core strands.

««««««««««««««««««««««««««««««««««»»»»»»»»»»»»»»»»»»»»»»»»»»»»»»»»»»»»

GATOR TAIL SINNET

An alligator tail has a series of tall ridges running along its tail. The GATOR TAIL SINNET uses a series of slip knots to create this design. This sinnet can store a large amount of paracord in its compact design. The slip knots on the bottom of this design are made in the opposite direction as the slip knots on the top.
To pull apart, pull on side straps.

Sinnet Material Equation: One 15 feet light cord + One 15 feet dark cord = 7.25 inch bracelet

1. Make a loop, clockwise *O* from left to right, in the middle of the dark cord. Lay the middle of the second light cord next to the loop.
2. Bend then pull the left dark cord over the second cord and through the loop.
3. Tighten the knot and adjust the cord to make a 0.5 inch loop.

4. Make a counter-clockwise loop with the right light cord then bend and pull the right cord under and through itself.
5. Tighten the knot.
6. Make a counter-clockwise loop with the left dark cord then bend and pull the right cord over and through itself.

7. Tighten the knot.
8. Make a clockwise loop with the left light cord then bend and pull the right cord under and through itself.
9. Tighten the knot.

10. Make a clockwise loop with the left dark cord then bend and pull the right cord over and through itself.
11. Tighten the knot. Adjust the slip knots with the dark loops on top and light on the bottom.
12. With the bottom right light cord, lasso the top right dark cord.

13. Tighten the bottom right cord.
14. With the bottom left light cord, lasso the top left dark cord.
15. Tighten the bottom left cord.

16. Pull the right dark loop through the left dark loop.
17. Tighten the dark cord on the left.
18. Make a clockwise loop with the left light cord then bend and pull the right cord under and through itself.

19. Tighten the knot.
20. Make a clockwise loop with the left dark cord then bend and pull the right cord over and through itself.
21. Tighten the knot.

22. With the bottom left light cord, lasso the top left dark cord.
23. Tighten the bottom left light cord.
24. Push down, or pinch, the knots when tightening to ensure design geometry. Pull the left dark loop through the right dark loop.

25. Tighten the dark cord on the right.
26. Make a counter-clockwise loop with the right light cord then bend and pull the right cord under and through itself.
27. Tighten the knot.

28. Make a counter-clockwise loop with the left dark cord then bend and pull the right cord over and through itself.
29. Tighten the knot.
30. With the bottom right light cord, lasso the top right dark cord.

31. Tighten the bottom right light cord.
32. Pull the right dark loop through the left dark loop.
33. Tighten the dark cord on the left.

34. Continue the pattern to the desired length.
35. Insert the cord ends through the loop.
36. Tighten the last loop to secure the cord ends.

37. Make a Stopper Knot (refer to pages 1 through 3), cut the ends and do NOT singe. Leave ends open for quick access to the core strands.

««»»

GATORBACK SINNET

Alligators have a series of ridges running along their back. The GATORBACK SINNET uses a series of slip knots to create this design. This sinnet can store a large amount of paracord in its compact design. The GATORBACK is a variation of the GATOR TAIL SINNET. The bottom slip knots are made in the same direction as the top slip knots. To pull apart, pull on side straps.

Sinnet Material Equation: One 15 feet light cord + One 15 feet dark cord = 7.25 inch bracelet

1. Make a loop, clockwise *O* from left to right, in the middle of the dark cord. Lay the middle of the second light cord next to the loop.
2. Bend then pull the left dark cord over the second cord and through the loop.
3. Tighten the slip knot and adjust the cord to make a 0.5 inch loop.

4. Make a counter-clockwise loop with the right top dark cord then bend and pull the right cord over and through itself.
5. Tighten the knot.
6. Make a counter-clockwise loop with the right bottom light cord then bend and pull the right cord over and through itself.

7. Tighten the knot.
8. Make a clockwise loop with the left top dark cord then bend and pull the right cord over and through itself.
9. Tighten the knot.

10. Make a clockwise loop with the bottom top light cord then bend and pull the right cord over and through itself.
11. Tighten the knot.
12. Adjust the slip knots with alternating light and dark colors.

13. With the bottom right dark cord, lasso the top right light cord.
14. Tighten the bottom right dark knot.
15. With the bottom left light cord, lasso the top left dark cord.

16. Tighten the bottom left light knot.
17. Pull the right light loop knot through the left dark loop.
18. Tighten the left dark cord.

19. Make a clockwise loop with the left top dark cord then bend and pull the right cord over and through itself.
20. Tighten the knot.
21. Make a clockwise loop with the bottom top light cord then bend and pull the right cord over and through itself.

22. Tighten the knot.
23. With the bottom left light cord, lasso the top left dark cord.
24. Tighten the bottom light knot.

25. Pull the left dark loop through the right light loop.
26. Tighten the right light cord.
27. Make a counter-clockwise loop with the right bottom dark cord then bend and pull the right cord over and through itself.

28. Tighten the knot.
29. Make a counter-clockwise loop with the right top light cord then bend and pull the right cord over and through itself.
30. Tighten the knot.

31. With the bottom right dark cord, lasso the top right light cord.
32. Tighten the bottom right dark cord.
33. Pull the right light loop through the left dark loop.

34. Tighten the left dark cord.
35. Push down, or pinch, the knots when tightening to ensure design geometry.
36. Continue the pattern to the desired length.

37. Insert the cord ends through the loop.
38. Tighten the last loop to secure the cord ends.
39. Make a Stopper Knot (refer to pages 1 through 3), cut the ends and do NOT singe. Leave ends open for quick access to the core strands.

«««««««««««««««««««««««««««««««««««««««»»»

S.H.T.F. SINNET

There is a basic philosophy or belief among preppers or survivalists. It is based on history repeating itself. Economies and governments will fail; Rome in 4 A.D., Spain in 1600s A.D. So, one should always be ready when S.H.T.F.! The S.H.T.F. SINNET can store a large amount of paracord in its design. It is a back-to-back design based on the RIPCORD SINNET. To pull apart, pull on each strap or both straps on each side.

Sinnet Material Equation: One 14 feet light cord + One 14 feet dark cord = 7.25 inch bracelet

1. Make a loop, clockwise *O* from left to right, in the middle of the dark cord.
2. Lay the middle of the second light cord next to the loop.
3. Bend then pull the left dark cord over the second light cord and through the loop.

4. Tighten the slip knot and adjust the cord to make a 0.5 inch loop.
5. Make a counter-clockwise loop with the right top dark cord then bend and pull the right cord over and through itself.
6. Tighten the knot.

7. Make a counter-clockwise loop with the right light cord then bend and pull the right cord under and through itself.
8. Tighten the knot.
9. Make a clockwise loop with the left light cord then bend and pull the left cord under and through itself.

10. Tighten the knot.
11. Make a clockwise loop with the left top dark cord then bend and pull the left cord over and through itself.
12. Tighten the knot.

13. Adjust the slip knots with the dark loops on top and light on the bottom.
14. Pull the two left slip knots through the two right loops.
15. To keep the first loop from adjusting, one can put a finger in the loop while tightening other knots.

16. Tighten the cords on the right.
17. Make a counter-clockwise loop with the right light cord then bend and pull the right cord under and through itself.
18. Tighten the knot.

19. Make a counter-clockwise loop with the right top dark cord then bend and pull the right cord over and through itself.
20. Tighten the knot.
21. Pull the two right slip knots through the two left loops.

22. Tighten the cords on the left.
23. Make a clockwise loop with the left light cord then bend and pull the left cord under and through itself.
24. Tighten the knot.

25. Make a clockwise loop with the left top dark cord then bend and pull the left cord over and through itself.
26. Tighten the knot.
27. Pull the two left slip knots through the two right loops.

28. Tighten the cords on the right.
29. Make a counter-clockwise loop with the right light cord then bend and pull the right cord under and through itself.
30. Tighten the knot.

31. Make a counter-clockwise loop with the right top dark cord then bend and pull the right cord over and through itself.
32. Tighten the knot.
33. Pull the two right slip knots through the two left loops.

34. Tighten the cords on the left.
35. Continue the pattern to the desired length.
36. Insert the cord ends through the loop.

37. Tighten the last loop to secure the cord ends.
38. Make a Stopper Knot (refer to pages 1 through 3), cut the ends and do NOT singe. Leave ends open for quick access to the core strands.

BIBLIOGRAPHY

American Preppers Network, *http://americanpreppersnetwork.com/,* 2013.

Ashley, Clifford W. *Ashley Book of Knots*, New York, Doubleday, 1944.

BFRO. Bigfoot Research Organization, *www.bfro.net*, 2013.

Budworth, Geoffrey. *The Complete Book of Decorative Knots*, London, Hamlyn, 1998.

Chimera*, http://en.wikipedia.org/wiki/Chimera_(genetics),* 2013

Finding Bigfoot, *http://animal.discovery.com/tv-shows/finding-bigfoot,* 2013.

Grainger, Stuart. *Creative Ropecraft, 4th Edition,* Dobbs Ferry, NY, Sheridan House, 2000.

Hillbilly Handfishin', *http://animal.discovery.com/tv-shows/hillbilly-handfishin/about-this-show/about-hillbilly-handfishin.htm,* 2013.

Lenzen, .J.D. *Tying It All Together, https://www.youtube.com/user/TyingItAllTogether/videos,* 2013.

Patriot Nurse, The *Patriot Nurse, http://www.youtube.com/user/ThePatriotNurse,* 2013.

Rhodesian Ridgeback, *http://www.akc.org/breeds/rhodesian_ridgeback/index.cfm,* 2013.

Shaw, John. *The Directory of Knots: a Step-by-Step Guide to Tying Knots*, New York, Metro Books, 2009.

Urban, Richard. *10 Fascinating Economic Collapses Through History, http://listverse.com/2012/12/26/10-fascinating-economic-collapses-through-history/* , 2012

Made in United States
Orlando, FL
27 August 2022